TRIALS AND TRIUMPHS

Kim Doran

First published by Kim Doran. 11/2022

ISBN#978-1-7369581-2-4

Cover Design by Tiffany Lynch

Author Photo by Lisa Berry

Printed in the United States of America

Trials and Triumphs

Kim's collection of poetry covering the trials and experiences that some of us go through, offers a unique glimpse into life. From the childlike, simple joy of jumping in puddles to the recount of fear in a child's abuse, Kim's words imprint the feelings into our minds. We feel the raindrops, the warm kiss of sunshine on our faces and yet, we feel the raw pain stab at us too. This collection brought it home for me so strongly, that we all need to offer grace to one another. As we never know what someone is overcoming from their past or currently.

God is there for us at our lowest points and our highest peaks. Seek Him in all areas of your life. Weave His name into your very being. Feel His healing peace wash over you.

Pauline Butler
Certified Christian Counselor
Retired RN

Dedicated to:

Paul Doran

You have stood by my side, through every obstacle and still stand holding my hand and cheering me on.

Thank you, love of my life, husband, best friend, every day in every way.

Contents

Trial — A person, thing, or situation that tests a person's endurance or forbearance

Triumph — A great victory or achievement

Definitions taken from Webster Dictionary

Trials and Triumphs

Captivity

Captivity is a state of mind
Got to rise up and leave it behind

It will hold you down, hold you back
There's more to do, cannot settle for that

Put one foot in front of the other
There's better, my sisters and brothers

Start in this moment, change comes today
Don't stay stuck, thumbs up to a new way

Situations in this world do harm
Filling up our minds, sounding off alarms

And captivity we all will come to face
As it runs throughout the human race

Yet, don't stay stuck in a darkened cave
Use the tools given, armor up - be brave

With trust, firm to stand in battle
See the enemy shake, run and rattle

In The Moment

A child sees
A child smiles
Just happy to be
In the moment
Small, so free

A child laughs
A child speaks
Just glad to be
In the moment
Young, with spree

A child hurts
A child cries
Just sad to be
In the moment
Tired, no glee

A child sleeps
A child dreams
Just gentle to be
In the moment
Beauty to see

Cycle

Traffic – it slows
        it speeds
        it stops

Sometimes smoothly
Sometimes recklessly
Sometimes without thought

Road Blocks – with detours
             with delays
             with pile ups

Occurs in day
Occurs in night
Occurs yet again

Life – it happens
     it hurts
     it thrives

Sometimes smoothly
Sometimes recklessly
Sometimes without thought

Death – with calm
       with pain
       with doubt

Occurs in day
Occurs in night
Occurs yet again

Rubber Boots

Lil rubber boots
Remind me of you
Thumping along – puddles
Singing while you do

Skies are dripping
Drops falling too
Jumping along – splashing
Laughing while you do

Lil rubber boots
Remind me of you
Growing along – walking
Talking while you do

Storms come often
Hurricanes come too
Moving along – living
Learning while you do

Lil rubber boots
Remind me of you
Lil rubber boots
You long outgrew

Await

Sound of the clock ticks
Oxygen flows and goes hiss
Your voice a gentle wisp
Tender eyes - release mist

Quiet time to just wait
Body and mind linger fate
Inner peace love equates
Final hours – await the great

Sleepy state of medicated bliss
In and out without a miss
Hands and feet dance lil bits
Talking up – blowing kiss

Rain pours from the sky
Body lays waiting to die
Nothing left to say or try
Choking back – goodbyes

The time now is nearing
You are without fearing
When eyes open in staring
The heavens start cheering

It

It started with a little gadget
That small box we hold in hands
It opened a world that invades
Fills the mind with sin of man

It draws in, shows many things
Sends it out among the mass
Exploiting with images and words
And ruins the lives of all class

It eats up time, creates emotions
Feel rejected - became the story
Images don't lie and all do see
Once it's out forget about sorry

It's the devil's tool used to harm
That all in one idol, the cell phone
Too much access too much sharing
Watch the turmoil become known

It is an addiction this small device
That we can't seem to put down
Hours spent scrolling time ticks away
Then we see it, our business and frown

It keeps us coming back for more
People, places, things we want to explore
It sucks us in to upgrade each year
All our dirty laundry posted and stored

Creek

The rushing water flows over the bend
Sweet melody of a caressing wind

The current goes smoothly by like time
Has nowhere to be, it cannot lie

Feels right standing here in this place
Nature's noise taking up head space

Go on, flow creek both long and wide
With beauty to outline on every side

Want to jump in and splash my feet
As the thrill of your magnitude is deep

Plunged in, soaking all of me
So refreshing and renewal complete

Slider

There's a snake in the garden
Who wants to be seen
Slithering all around
Acting like a queen

Not caring about territory
Or who she bites
Got an agenda
Looking for a fight

Beware of the slider
She will strike and hurt
Has her plan in motion
Will leave you in dirt

So pick up your sword
Use it when you must
Cry out a prayer plea
Watch snake turn to dust

All

Lay it down
All that weighs heavy
Upon mind and shoulders
Burdens carried too long

Hand it over
All the unrest found
Filling heart and soul
Anchors holding too strong

Lift it up
All that consumes
Stealing time and hope
Chains rattling so wrong

Give it away
All that needs riddance
Upon and within
Freedom to belong

A Soldier For God

There he stood tall and proud
Armed with a bible in hand
A cross hung on his neck

His confidence quite clear
Within his humbleness
No doubt, not even a speck

Words he spoke of truth
Belief in it with ease
Delivered with respect

He told the written word
Steady with scripture's plan
Temptations he'd expect

There he stood firm and sound
A soldier for God
His duty never to neglect

His armor strong and secure
For God, the only One
All others he'd reject

The Table

The kitchen cozy and ready to fill
A welcome to all, yet still
Someone won't come out of pride
Holding hurts for a long ride

The table is long, love inviting
A seat with your name providing
Some encourage, some say don't go
But if you decline, you won't know

This home is not full without you
A place designed to be true
Regardless of regrets and mistakes
This kitchen can be a healing space

This table is ready to be full
Laughter and tears never dull
Come on home, let us hug you
Forgiveness given, intentional truth

Keeping

Snarled up in the day to day
All the thoughts get in the way
Where to go – what to say
Keeping true feelings at bay

Knotted down root to surface
Chasing after the golden purpose
Why here - why service?
Keeping emotions the furthest

Scrunched up with limited room
To spread about and bloom
How to grow – how to groom
Keeping tabs on the doom

Crowded from ground to sky
Smothered in all the lies
Want to be – want to cry
Keeping safe behind the eyes

Here To There

From here to there
Feels so long, so far
Each step closer
To where you are

The field is big
Graced by wind, by sun
A path to walk
Jump, laugh and run

From here to there
Steps to take, to gait
Drawing me closer
Direction of pure fate

Body At Work

It came
In the form
Of helping hands
With no agenda
No expectation
Other than to reach to touch my soul

Sent to
Assist in need
Willing and able
With no boast
No brag
Just to be hands to feed my heart

Stepped up
Came to aid
Strong and armed
With no hustle
No barter
Just feet to stand to open my mind

To be
Body at work
In His name
With no applause
No limelight
Only to express kindness to leap my joy

Click

Click Click Click
Send it Send it
I won't share it
I promise

No No No
I can't I can't
Will only you see
You promise?

Images not meant
For eyes to see
Pics of flesh
Of you and me

How exciting
Yet feels wrong
Exposure experienced
Feel so strong

Nervous laughter
Showing our stuff
Giggles and gasping
Calling our bluff

Click Click Click
Send more Send more
I will delete
I promise

Ok Ok Ok
Are you sure Are you sure
It's just for you
You promise?

Images go viral
All eyes do see
Photos of her
All his delete

How shocking
It's so bad
Naked and scared
Feel so had

Shameful heart
Head held low
Finger pointing
Cruel name calling

Click Click Click
One more One more
Girl found dead
Totally defeated

Gone Gone Gone
Too soon Too soon
He destroyed her
Broken promise

Pace

Today may not go as planned
But trust you are in His hands

For the way you think you are to go
May not be what you need to grow

Move at a pace that allows change
Much opportunity is not estranged

Stop the in warped speed of your mind
True experience you will come to find

There is a lot that needs to get done
And it will in due time from the One

Today is now, in this very second
Open your ears up and hear the beckon

Seasons Change

No less beautiful as petals fall from stems
Just as gorgeous from beginning to end

So gentle yet strong in all life's spaces
The soft and hardness of earthly places

Underneath has become willingly visible
In precious moments love indivisible

As growth occurs and the seasons change
Providing a masterpiece within range

Worn

She stands at the picket fence
Not wanting to step closer
A house filled with strangers
Where no one even knows her

Removed from her parents' home
The allegations were true
Signs of physical abuse
It seemed everyone knew

Social services stepped on in
Determined to take a stand
Pulling her out of chaos
Into a strange man's hand

From one place of bad behavior
To another of sheer pain
A young girl taken against will
Tears spill out like pouring rain

How does one make sense of it?
A blameless child used to please
Sinful lusters living in greed
A soft pat, a touch, a squeeze

This child in need of rescue
A different place to be found
To spare her body and mind
Where secure love is around

Standing at another gate
Her small body starts to shake
What awaits her in this place?
Outer images are so fake

The white picket fence is tall
Beyond it is the unknown
Been passed around like left-overs
What is the meaning of home?

Shaking turns into panic
Her hand held and led forward
The door opens with a smile
Her crying eyes lowered

Not trusting in this instant
She pulls away uncertain
For so much pain she has had
Living a heavy burden

Steps back from the strange face
An inch given and she ran
Rushing down the narrow road
Just cannot do it again

Racing away from another trap
Stained cheeks puff with hard breath
A hand lands on her overcoat
Her body tenses with dread

Eyes centered on this stranger
Not believing in this plan
Fearing yet another scam
Born to this world of lost man

A soft voice like no other
Soothes the hurt she feels inside
Sensing this time is different
As her mind and heart collide

Falling on her worn out knees
Pointing her face to the sky
Calling on the Lord who saves
Asking to be lifted high

This life has been dark and torn
Many nights not left alone
No one to ease all the pain
Only faces of hard stone

Knowing one day it would end
For He has come to amaze
With her now, this very day
Her trust in the Lord to save

The time of freedom has come
Now she lives not an illusion
The blessing of the Lord's hands
Has granted her absolution

Claire's story

Rainbow

Storms come
Storms go
The scars it leaves sometimes don't show

Clouded over
Clouded under
The reality booms ironclad thunder

Downpour strikes
Downpour floods
Hearts torn apart over spilled blood

Rainbow forms
Rainbow reminds
The struggles overcome when faith intertwines

Now

Right now is new
Nothing you can do

Yesterday is gone
That time is done

Come let it go
Strength it shows

Step forward now
Have faith is how

Don't carry baggage
Lay down the damage

Grasp a new start
Now do your part

Fragrance

The sweet fragrance
Blows upon us
His breath filling
Opening up life
So gentle – so mighty
Firm yet loving
Cleansing sin and strife

The fresh breeze
Comes upon us
His breath brings
A new hope
So soft – so true
Hard yet merciful
Beyond, be and cope

The sweet fragrance
Fills old bones
His Holy Spirit
Breathes in us
So pure – so good
Direct yet calming
Restoring frail and rust

Get Out Get Off

Get out of my head
Get off my limbs
You try to drown me
But I will swim instead

You have no authority
You must flee
You can try, try
But you won't conquer me

Get out of my head
Get off my limbs
You try to sink me
But I will swim

I know your games
It is all lies
Distorted and turned
Festering up ties

Get out of my head
Get off my limbs
You try to flood me
But I will swim

I called on the power
The Almighty above all
He knows your plot
You will soon fall

Born to Save

A baby boy wrapped in cloth
Entered this world filled with void
Little to no helping hands
Showed the hearts of fallen man

Yet God shared His splendor
When He gifted us with His son
For Jesus became the great defender
Of lost souls - our shame undone

Jesus grew and shared the Word
Walked in love, with mercy and grace
From city to city and land to land
To fulfill His Father's ultimate plan

But human is as human does
Mankind returned His love with stain
Disbelief and ridicule, toxic behavior
Persecuted our true king, our Savior

God made that heartbreaking sacrifice
For us all to stand right here today
Jesus took the nails, tears upon His face
His blood spilt to save the whole race

His words became truth for us to see
As His body lay wrapped in linens
In a darken tomb sealed by rock
Yet, didn't prevent His return to His flock

And on the third day He was risen
Seen by Mary Magdalene, she spread the news
A visit to the disciples confirmed the truth
Jesus, King of kings will always rule

His resurrection brought us a new start
As His living water flows in our hearts
Spread the Word His promises are true
Now disciples go do as He instructed you

Agony

Walls before
Ceilings low
Bars holding
Want to let go

Noise loud
Feelings torn
Grip tightens
Want to be re-born

Feet shackled
Hands cuffed
Life taken
Don't want this stuff

Choices made
Time inside
Price paid
Don't want to die

Mind wanders
Reality sets
Voice whispers
Want no regrets

Heart hurts
Body lays
Locked up
Want a new way

Seeking now
Being still
Praying out
Don't want my will

Quiet moment
Staring ahead
In waiting
Don't want this dread

Crying loud
Tears swell
Deep agony
Want to rid hell

Constant shaking
Eager pleading
Remorseful words
Want becomes needing

Light

The way is lit by a light
That brings inner delight
For there is no bulb, no switch
And it is without any glitch

It burns constant and bright
Through morning and night
Illuminating the way we take
From dry land to smooth lake

Shimmer for the eye to see
Beaming within you and me
The way has been laid out
For us to walk not in doubt

Light came for all to know
A guiding hand to show
Freely lifted above all sin
For in the end, light does win

No Sinking

The bow of my ship
Never went under
Even when my head
Was filled with thunder

I plunged into depth
Just needing to know
What it was ahead
Released all control

The sails were tattered
Shifted all around
As life's wind blew
A bellowing sound

I held on so tight
Hands gripped the wheel
Directly facing the storm
My mind an open reel

The bow took a hit
Yet, up it came
Battled the flooding
No sand now remained

On a solid rock built
No sinking occurred
Faithful redeemer
My sins He incurred

Photo

The photo touched me deeply today
I am not sure why
Read the words and saw the image
I started to cry
How often was I at that point in time
Without support yet, quite sublime

The photo wrecked me greatly today
I am so sure why
Read the words and saw the image
I wanted to deny
That was me and sometimes still is
Dangling by thread, easily dismissed

Reflections of You, Reflections of Me

In my quietness
You walk with me and show
Reflections of You, reflections of me

In my loneliness
You fill me and show
Reflections of You, reflections of me

In my torment
You hold me and show
Reflections of You, reflections of me

In my surrender
You lift me and show
Reflections of You, reflections of me

In my longing
You are near me and show
Reflections of You, reflections of me

In my wholeness
You complete me and show
Reflections of You, reflections of me

Fear

It may look like the road to nowhere
But rest assured it goes somewhere

Fear like bumps all along the way
Especially when you must face today

Sights and sounds can be alarming
Yet, surroundings are quite charming

Walking, running, driving down the path
Looking around left to right, think fast

Hard to enjoy the beauty of it all
When in fact you feel lost and small

The road ahead leads to unknown
Start praying now as you are alone

Sweaty fingers grip tight the wheel
Wanting to turn around and bail

But, on you press talking to self
Begging the Lord to show himself

The GPS dings, you have arrived
It's then you realize, you have survived

Ground Bound

Out of the dark box they hop
Inhaling in the fresh air
Feeling her hand touch their skin
Anxious to go somewhere

Wanting her to take them home
So tired of being alone
Hoping she likes pretty blues
And all the sparkling stones

It would be harsh and so cruel
If placed back in the tomb
Oh so eager to be free
Want to smell life's perfume

Seeing her look on over
Feel her feet slip in them
Their excitement starts to build
Bringing to life their gems

Being out of the dark box
Is where they want to be
Exploring the world at large
To play, dance and to see

Knowing it is up to her
Whether the fit is right
As she walks back and forth
They sparkle with delight

Tension creates laces tight
Down she looks at her feet
Colors and gems at full tilt
Smiling she speaks "so sweet"

Up to the counter she goes
They squirm because they know
Life is about to begin
She freed them from death's row

The Walk

The walk is long, sometimes straight, sometimes not
View may be incredible or can be jaded and dark
And if you stop from time to time you'll see a lot
Sightings may bring fear or ignite a spark

The walk is hard, sometimes good ,sometimes bad
Scene may be majestic or can be fog stirred
And if you stop from time to time you will feel rad
Canvas may be full of life or slightly blurred

The walk is good, sometimes warm, sometimes cold
Vastness may be welcomed or can be denied
And if you stop from time to time you'll find bold
The path may restore or be full of pride

The walk is waiting, sometime between now and later
Steps may be slow or can be super fast
And if you stop from time to time you meet the creator
The walk will change your very life, be found at last

Resigned

Our home is tucked away
Where life we spend many days
With much joy and yes sorrows
Gets us through the tomorrows

Nestled deep among the trees
Beauty as far as eyes can see
Better hearts now in this clan
Resigned of the worldly plan

Do Not

Do not envy me
For I share freely
Do not pity me
For I shall overcome

Walk with me instead
As we are friends
Walk with exuberant step
Light up and represent

Do not speak death
It's a waste of breath
Do not wish me harm
Explore my kind charm

Talk only to me true
All we have been through
Talk of common ground
And my heart you found

Do not tear down
Creates a sad frown
Do not live in vain
Surely nothing to gain

Live full of hope
Step off slippery slope
Live full- live free
All to see and be

Each

We are all so very different yet, placed here to interact
Some will have things in common and some will retract

Each made according to the mighty One's master plan
Each one of us, every child, woman and man

Blended in this vast and diverse place called earth
Everyday someone fighting for what it's worth

We are all so very different yet, much the same
With outer appearences, a dude or a dame

With blood that bleeds and hearts that break
Some always give and some simply will take

3

My first day free into the world
Sweet baby girl – life's plan swirled
Home not with mother and father
Placed instead in arms of another

Strangers took responsibility for me
A newborn - with a crying plea
Orphanage, my early nesting place
One of many in this crowded space

Open seas and in midst of a war
Landed me on a distant shore
Illness and malnutrition riddled me
Unknown loving hands was what I see

Was cared for, then sent me away
To a family stationed at bay
The odds worked in my favor
Miracles far and few, one to savor

Now a toddler bouncing around
Along came another, a precious sound
Welcomed me and baby brother too
Young lives freed from certain doom

To the states we did come
A blended family and then some
Another baby boy adopted, now safe
And no longer be left in waif

These two people became our world
3 different children, two boys and a girl
They opened their hearts, called us in
This family united for a win win

We waved the flag, said the pledge
So very blessed to beat the alternative – dead
Military life moved us all around
Our young hearts and minds profound

We grew in love, we stayed together
Our bonded family through all weather
Just when I could not feel any better
An unexpected came in form of a letter

I was now grown and living well
An added bonus this news would tell
See I had some more family
And they sought me out hastily

From my birth land so far away
Records tracked and led to this day
Siblings who were blood to me
Found they had a baby sister absentee

In the states they too had grown
With parents that were my own
Mom and dad lived no longer
Rose above and became stronger

They found a way to find
The little sister left behind
The one of 3 born unfree
Eager to come and welcome me

Now I thought of all that occurred
And I plunged into faith – Word
Born German adopted Jewish- oh wow
Our God moves – to Him I bow

Life had many ups and downs
Yet I am grateful to be around
Love has come and filled me up
God's blessings continue to fill my cup

A man to love and to be loved
A home provided from above
With 3 more we welcomed in
Caring hearts raising our grandchildren

Things have a way of coming full circle
For I am one of triples
As in Father, Son and Holy Spirit
My journey is with great merit

Born 3 is my biology
Adopted 3 was my destiny
Welcomed 3 that belonged with me

Lisa's story

Fractured

The tiny crack
Runs through head
Down to toes
It expands daily
Piercing the heart
No one knows

It moves deeper
Grows longer still
Throughout all
Crushing the soul
Won't let go
All hope falls

The tiny crack
Started long ago
Yet patched up
Eyes can't see
Breaking the heart
Dried up cup

It seeps slowly
Tainting all veins
Taking control
Living in pain
Fractured inner self
No one knows

Dwell

The space that fills
Dwells within
Below skin level
Unseen by eyes
Yet visible
In actions, in words

The knowing that is
Wrapped up
Dangled around core
Holding loosely on
Yet firm
In truth, in promise

The breath that comes
Filling up
Lungs to sing
Glory to give
Ever strong
In spirit, in reverence

The life freely lived
Standing here
Hands and feet
Eyes are open
Yet narrow
In focus, in faith

Soak

Rain splats
Soaks the streets
Wind whistles
Its own tune

Trees bend
Branches fall off
Birds hide
In tiny nest

Puddles grow
Run like streams
Thunder booms
In the storm

Lightning cracks
In the sky
Downpour comes
And soaks all

Stars fade
Night is dark
Time lingers
And holds captive

Morning breaks
Light filters in
Calm now
And breathe again

Wait

Don't knock me down for you are walking through a valley
Just trust that I have been there too
I wait on the other side with a hand outstretched to you

Don't turn away a voice of wisdom for you choose unwisely
Just know that I have run before blindly
I wait on the other side with a hug for you kindly

Don't wave off a word of truth for you can't take anymore
Just think that I have been there too
I wait on the other side with hope you choose to walk through

Paths

Wrong to right
Dark to light
Air in our lungs
Speak life with tongues

Day and night
Black and white
Together in this place
Filling up space

Weak and strong
Short and long
Paths made to follow
Without being shallow

Here and now
Today and tomorrow
Feet now get moving
A revival is brewing

Felt Like

The tightening of my vocal chords
With the pressure of invisible hands
That's what it felt like in that moment
When you told me I did not matter

The air restricted, no flow through
With the grip of angered fingers
That's what it felt like in that moment
When you told me I was a liar

Then the bulb in my mind clicked on
Declaring your words were very wrong
That's what it felt like in that moment
When I told you to be gone

Affinity came fast upon all of me
Allowing my heart to beat freely
That's what it felt like in that moment
When I told you of my victory

Imprinted

Behind the anguish is something good to see
Yet the memories keeping flooding my mind
And getting the best and worst of me
Offering glimpses of hope I try to find

What was, is no more, my view obscured
Tugging on my heart strings, thoughts roaming
Picking up pieces of self off the floor
With flashbacks of us in love condoning

Oh the fiery sky like the depths of hearts
Burning in opposite directions, yet colliding
And strumming a tune that hits the mark
No answers, love lost in ultimate dividing

Despite the endless ache one can look ahead
Through the brush and fallen limbs to see
Get a dose, reality of temporary tread
Lesson in love clearly imprinted for you and me

Happened

He stood alone
Staring at phone
Hearing the laughter
Awaiting a disaster

She stood still
Tears easily spilt
Hearing the threats
Of harmful mindsets

It happened once, it will happen again

He lifted head
Mind misled
Arched his back
Ready to attack

She turned around
Making no sound
Body took stance
End dark romance

It happened once, it will happen again

He took charge
To stop barrage
Finish their game
Wild, now tamed

She rose up
Faced the club
Spoke with vigor
Pulled the trigger

It happened once, it won't happen again

Darkness

Darkness actually cannot win
Unless you cave and let it in
It longs to take hold, not let go
Desires to conquer your soul

Moving in with full intent
Total destruction is meant
To take all, that you are
Pull your heart, toss it far

Weakness it seeks in you
Reeking havoc in all you do
Not willing to chance, or lose
Nor let you think and choose

Darkness in itself has no claim
Unless you let it take aim
Without you, giving consent
It will surely stay hell bent

Twisted Fate

Infatuated, manipulated, unsure
Looking for love, opened door
Premonitions are so strong
This is gunna go wrong

The road ahead looks great
Yet it could be twisted fate
Intentions are not quite clear
Got you walking in beware

Hidden, forbidden, impure
Thoughts overloaded, insecure
Craving is taking charge
Outburst fully enlarged

The road back holds strain
From choices, made in derange
Time to heal the wounds
So old ways never resume

Roam

You drive around with nowhere to go
Needing to think, hours alone
Fearing what you have called home
So out on the road you roam

The quiet night hides your face
As the tears fall out in place
Your heart hurts, begins to race
With all you feel disgraced

Without direction you just drive
Wondering how you're still alive
Deep inside extrication strives
Groan of affliction throat cries

You drive not wanting to go
Feeling safer when all alone
And longing to avoid home
Out on the road you still roam

Glance

The window exposed the life outside
While rest and solace laid inside
The river flowed in constant tempo
Trees swayed like breath letting go

This hazy day felt appropriate
Reminder of life as we know it
Her body lay in place peering out
With no expression nor words about

Birds of every color flew and danced
That sweet dragonfly gave a glance
They came together to let us know
Despite somber, we are never alone

A slight smile and an ever soft hum
Pulled on my heart, the time has come
To surrender the physical seen here
Simply trust that transition's near

No more struggle, no sorrow or pain
The skies opened up with cleansing rain
A humble servant newly renamed
Taken home, her salvation proclaimed

Post

Held in hand
In morning- at night
All through the day, insane

Got to see
Who – what
Every minute craves

Time ticks away
Seconds – minutes
Eating up the clock

Battery burns down
Plug in – then peek
See what was missed

Post the good
Hide the bad
Addiction is sustained

Celebrations are shared
All smiles – all right
Bliss is all around

Tragedy brings pain
Many prayers – many tears
Cry out desperation

Gadget in hand
Eyes on fingers - scroll
Time to let go

Events are displayed
Invited – not invited
Obligation or blues

Post the truth
In morning – at night
All through the day, insane

Reminder

The holes in your hand and feet
Remind me
You, alone took to that cross
Never to walk in defeat

Spread love across all barriers
That were meant to destroy
But it just cannot out beat
The depth of You without decoy

The scars seen on my body
Remind me
You, alone are most holy
Always giving so freely

Sharing life across all borders
Chasing out the evil reaper
Faith is growing much stronger
Into levels beyond deeper

Broken Vessel No More

I am a willing vessel this day
Just as I was all the years back then
Living the faith life - a simple way
When home meant family led by men

God fearing parents taught us well
To talk the talk and walk the walk
Through youth and school-trying to avoid hell
Life was good as one of the chosen flock

When love bloomed for this young girl
I accepted his ring still in high school
Many plans had my head in a whirl
But chance would have it, his actions uncool

Messed around, broke the golden rule
Heart crushed, mind thinking, "I am not enough"
Set off a belief system, like hot fuel
A new season of rough, bitter and gruff

Eighteen came, more pain, as daddy passed away
In my adolescent arms his last breath faded
Leaving my mama shattered, in such a stray
And my short years completely invaded

As turmoil kept on my young strained back
High school graduation, a major milestone
With a date, a party, an unwanted attack
Left me feeling damaged and utterly alone

I thought I knew who and what he was
But I was wrong, and harm was done
Surely taken for granted, all for his cause
Watched as he choked it up as some grad fun

For me it was the beginning of my end
The dreams, the goals all turned to dust
I hid from all, even my closet friends
Too ashamed and afraid, hide it I must

Buried it deep until the signs appeared
My growing belly, mentally ready to bust
So action I took despite all my fears
Against my faith I did the forbidden disgust

In a mere few months my life was lost
With much hurt inside I gave into depression
Drinking, drugging, easily triggered at any cost
Spiraling out of control, living hard lessons

Then came that friend, with obstacles, yet peace
She showed me how, to not bury, move on
Instead of stuffing it all away, just cease
Into treatment I went, more pros than cons

The issues I carried-addiction, heartache, anger
Shame and resentment, just to name a few
Had me wrapped up tight and pointing fingers
Recovery gave me the chance to start anew

Finally, a good man to love I did meet
We went and tied the knot and became one
With two precious daughters, yet still incomplete
Me not whole, his infidelity could not be undone

Bad memories came crashing back in
Of hurt, lies told and innocence stolen
Would I ever deserve love, would I ever win?
My hopes beaten down, hurts are swollen

Hindering all that had been hidden away
With years of hiding the rape, the shame
Was slowly eating at my soul every day
Of masking the truth, taking the blame

Peeling back the layers to expose the roots
And open up the closet to the brutal truth
Inner stomping and kicking with steel toe boots
Sin everywhere, painful events stole my youth

A third of my life I've been held in captivity
Decisions made, yet not imprisoned anymore
Changed my outlook from past to productivity
Gave my soul to the Lord, every fiber to the core

Celebrate Recovery helped me take a stand
Putting bits and pieces back together again
Watching transformation in His mighty hands
No more falling down the rabbit hole- Amen!

I am a willing vessel this current day
Just as I was long ago, back then
Yet, these days I am led in a new way
Guiding in love for all my broken friends

Kimberly's story

Comes To Be

I sit
I wait
As morning comes to be

I look
I see
All that's around me

I think
I wonder
Am I truly free?

I cry
I scream
Are you here?

I feel
I reach
Allow you in

I sit
I wait
As night comes to be

Like Life

The waves crash hard before me
Thrust of force cannot be denied
Like life that gets tumbled around
Hope's in sight on this unbalanced ride

Fierce sounds are all consuming
While racing in and falling back out
Like life that shakes and stirs abound
Faith fills heart and mind without doubts

The current moves with a steady flow
A cycle of motion under gallant grace
Like life that pulls forth unsteady ground
Mercy humbly given in this created place

The setting is alive with absolute beauty
As forces battle to claim the victory
Like life the ups and downs come rapidly
Charity at great lengths, a blessed story

Weary

I am weary not because life has struggles
But rather because emotions are juggled

Words spewed back and forth in reaction
As we all sit and watch the main attraction

Morals and common respect are utterly lost
As we allow society to flip and toss

And where is our heart for all of mankind
Instead we see groups on the rise to deny

That this given world was made for us all
As one body to come and stand up tall

Weary, I am and so are many of you
Watching in horror, new world order in view

Storm

Don't tell me
My tears for you
Should not flow
They are hard
They fall strong

I'm alone in the storm
Praying you through your own

Days so long
My heart's with you
Keeps beating on
Faster than light
Faster than norm

I'm alone in the storm
Yet praying you back home

Nights in unrest
My mind on you
Gnarled up inside
Full of stuff
Full of hurt

I'm alone in the storm
And you are already gone

See

The dark liar tries
At every angle
To block out
So you can't see
But there's no dark
Big enough to stop
The light abundant
And totally free

Don't let deceiver win
Reach up your hand
High and outstretched
And tell it to flee
Making only room
Clear vision to see
Light brings life
And is your destiny

Earthly Ties

I know you are tired of the pain
Anxiously waiting on He who reigns

This process is not at all appealing
Riddled in meds, out of control feeling

Moments of solitude then body jitters
As you become slowly withered

But, beyond what the eye can see
Is a new day bright as can be

Where the hardness you walked through
Will be of the past as you renew

Waiting is part of the way
Holding your life at bay

When the call comes you will rise
Letting go of all earthly ties

Leaving all behind without strife
Onto the promise of eternal life

Body, mind and soul now at peace
As your spirit is freely released

Target

Have you been blown away
From the pack
Because of engrossed self
Target on your back

Have you wandered so far
To find joy
In the midst of chaos
Now a play toy

Have you thought for a second
The torment caused
As you think of only you
Seeking to fix flaws

Have you forgotten what matters
As you run
Into the mess of another
And all that's done

Have you taken a chance
Where one consumes
The best of what you give
Only to be ruined

Have you lost your mind
Trying so hard
To grasp on in desperation
Armor down, off guard

Man Made Disease

Through the eyes of a boy
A man sized world to face
With no father around
His heart, an empty space

So many days spent longing
For love to make its mark
Mom stretched to her limit
His eyes, focused on dark

Confusion was no stranger
Daily turmoil filled his home
Abuse to the extreme
His body, trapped and alone

A blast from her fist
Mom often delivered
Words flew from her mouth
His life, unconsidered

Coping came to an end
So he took to the street
Lost and vulnerable
Stepping into deceit

Much in need to belong
Mean streets scooped him up
Using his innocence
Overflowing his cup

Pain and anger were replaced
With ignorant pride
This life he was living
Seemed destined to thrive

As darkness followed him
From boy to young man
His chosen remedy
Addiction took a stand

Poison rocked his body
Usage consumed his mind
Weighing all his options
Home's darkness left behind

Newly found friends guided
Lifting him up in glory
Now using and dealing
Just added to his story

Lost in all the pleasures
Living large on a whim
Different girls come and go
Yet, one stands out to him

Her love and compassion
The brightness on dark days
Filled in his empty space
Changed his unruly ways

But history crept on in
And unsettled his world
His old habits surfaced
Stranding his wife and girls

She cried out, how can you
Choose walking dead over life?
Watching a craving man
Battling, take another slice

Faith, her only keepsake
As she bows down to pray
Her husband living high
Another sadly wasted day

His eyes could not focus
On the love sent his way
Body ragged and useless
To his drugs he obeyed

With prayer an answer comes
To expose all the fears
To wash away the sins
Soothing the heartfelt tears

In the middle of certain failure
A true blessing appeared
Admittance to face it
And let the spirit seer

The endless fog lifted
Its grip revealing a man
Longing to truly live
Believing now he can

Knowing it will be tough
No easy road ahead
With sheer determination
Now to become undead

There just is not a fix
For the man made disease
Not found in a bottle
Or an angry release

His feet plantly firmly
He opened up his heart
Called on the Lord's mercy
Begging for a new start

The flood came so quickly
Pulled him down beneath
A program to free him
A taste of pure belief

He listened with intent
Unknown path felt right
His eyes fully opened
Given enlightened sight

With concerns of his past
Dismissed with a wave
Thanking the precious Lord
For today he is saved

A lost man now in bloom
Heart filled with gratitude
Man-made demons defeated
His darkened life renewed

Addiction is tough to beat
It holds close, takes squeeze
Off the path occurs easily
Any user would agree

He was no different than most
Fall he did fast and hard
Hurting everyone who believed
Messed up life, completely scarred

Family threw up their hands
Went from bad to the worst
Druggie ways came to claim
Kissed the ground face first

Left to die where he lay
Desperate cries still invade
Looking up his eyes saw
Full intact angel brigade

Knowing he was near death
His inner voice was heard
A promise to lay it down
Rock bottom moment occurred

Today he is a man on mission
Out on the streets sharing hope
His journey a battle to survive
Helping others toss the dope

M's story

Garden

The garden was so inviting
Every inch with a welcoming
That said come as you are
Yet, it sat empty, felt so far

The soft lights all twinkled
With scent of greenery enticing
A spot at the table awaited
A seat vacant, memory faded

The site was awkwardly serene
A picture of perfect peace
That said come as you are
Yet, it sat empty, under sky of stars

The soft lights went dim
The greenery heavy with dew
A table set, but unused
A lovely and lonely view

Too Soon

Stunned
Shocked
The wound is deep
As reality sets in
Knees weak
Tell me
Didn't hear those words
As heart bleeds
Catch me
In agony
Loss comes – grieve
Want not to believe
Life flashes
Childhood memories
Gone way too soon
Leaving me gloom
Crying
Surreal
Now totally broken
In all its truth
Longing
Fading
Time comes through
And gone too soon

Moves On

Water flows
Cleansing shows
Flood with control
And it moves on

Deep falls
Raining walls
Current on call
And it moves on

Stream way
New today
Tide will sway
And it moves on

Flow low
Path narrow
Surf grows
And it moves on

Your Treasure

Your love is spread across the land
Everything made, created by hand
You fill our eyes with amazing things
And allow our voices to readily sing

Your blood was spilt for our souls
To walk this earth in human roles
Yet your spirit keeps us moving on
Brains and bodies often so far gone

Your truth has us desiring more
Like children in a candy store
Eager to feel and dive right in
Wanting at all cost to know the win

Your blood flows pumping red
Letting us know we are not dead
You surely feed us what we need
Providing all the fruit and seed

Your mercy has us all in wonder
As we hear sounds of thunder
Fill us up with love beyond measure
Opened the door of Your treasure

Curtain

What the eye can see brings belief
Also a feeling, a sense of relief
However, down beyond the bend
Often fills with dismay instead

The life we walk is uncertain
Until we find, open the curtain
Along this path simply trust
The steps we take are a must

Some trials are out in the open
Lessons of life honestly spoken
Others happen behind closed doors
When hunched over on the floor

Actions lead the way, or perhaps stray
Can invite and welcome us to stay
With choices to make be certain
All is better with an open curtain

Old Chapters

When time stands still
No words can be said
Every muscle stiffened
No script to be read

Heart pumps extra hard
While you taste reality
Now forever changed
Different view in totality

Well onward you go
No sense looking back
What was, has changed
Undeniably that's a fact

Here's to moving ahead
Old chapters stored away
Preserved in memory
With new ground to lay

The Waiting Room

A place to sit
A place to think
As random thoughts
Creep around head - sink

People come and go
More to come and go
A revolving door
It's booming steady - flow

Faces are blank
Minds are somewhere
Sure not wanting
To be right – here

Not willing to give
An inch or concede
Avoiding eye contact
For it suggest – defeat

Yet warriors wait
Listening for name
Hearts beat fear
In this sickness - game

Tries to consume
Death unstoppable doom
But hope strives
On other side- waiting room

Crush

The breaking point
For some is closer
Than for others

Don't be one
That pushes so hard
They fall over

Life thin thread
Words pierce hearts
Sever off heads

Time is hard
So many are distant
Simply disregard

The struggle unknown
Lived by friends
Shuts them out

The truth bends
Actions crush spirits
Violence no mend

Toughest Miles

Your words came
But was unsure
If heard clear
Or mind's detour

Time was long
Prayer kept on
A message received
New plan born

Jumped into action
Sold the business
And home too
With great quickness

Hit the road
A familiar state
Set up home
Following our fate

All seemed well
Falling into place
Building a life
In blessed space

Home and jobs
Came within reach
Short time later
A hard teach

Gainful employment ceased
Ninety days in
Rocking our lives
Caught in whirlwind

Scared and alone
Strained to survive
Amped up worries
Hit by tide

The journey cracked
Our hearts open
On our knees
Prayers were spoken

What came next
We never foresaw
The rug pulled
Filled with flaw

Heath challenges surfaced
Bigger than ever
Visit to doctor
Declared an endeavor

An improper counsel
Caused severe damage
In medication lapses
Left me savage

System in shock
From changed plan
Brain played tricks
So it began

Sleep was sparse
Then the hallucinations
Lost motor skills
For the duration

Common things faded
Basic no more
Walking, eating, talking
Became someone's chore

Without anyone
To lend hand
Into a center
Sporting wrist band

Welcomed me in
Place for care
Around the clock
Aid to repair

The medication changes
Had caused demise
Another regiment given
With great surprise

The plan working
Time was healing
Mind/body feeling
Well care revealing

With renewed hope
The hurt subsided
Actions of past
Had left divided

Striving to overcome
Worked hard daily
Regaining my identity
Removed the scaly

Yet still more
As covid hit
Doors got locked
I threw fit

Could not see
Husband not permitted
Felt all distance
As was committed

Ups and downs
On various meds
Heart aching
Messed with head

Nurses gave care
Reading the Word
Encouraged my path
No longer blurred

Pressed on forward
Plunged into art
Took some steps
Did my part

Things came back
Movement in limbs
Speech improved
Released from grim

Without contact
I missed him
Husband was waiting
Time was slim

Restoration did happen
Thirty days in
Walked out door
We'd begin again

The track rough
Yet now freed
Off all meds
But one need

World was down
Illness took charge
Spent hours praying
Perspective enlarged

Still needed time
Progress was slow
Stayed in Word
Eager to grow

Limitations were set
Decisions then made
Sell the house
Easily swayed

Just like that
It sure went
Packed us up
Feeling quite content

Traveled back home
Start all over
Home and business
Mind/body sober

Friends were reclaimed
Helped us settle
Some challenges remained
Foot to pedal

Days got better
Sturdy and anew
God had healed
Much to do

My faith deepened
Beyond my understanding
Surrounded by angels
Under new branding

Life has flourished
Sickness no more
Walking in awe
He opened door

Restored and transformed
Living the dream
Meant to be
Child of supreme

Chains have fallen
Hold no longer
Road is clear
I am stronger

Know I walked
The toughest miles
To get here
Through the trials

Now I see
Not like before
All His love
I'm truly adored

Connie's story

Exposed

In between the clouds is a hiding place
Where shame and regret we don't face

It's there underneath the surface
Without seeking to find any purpose

It haunts as we keep it tucked away
Running in circles every single day

To avoid being exposed out in open
A badge of disgrace slowly choking

This choice to hide only consumes
The best parts concealing us in ruin

Peel back the clouds and shine through
Yesterday's gone and shouldn't stop you

Bones

Brittle bones
Laying dead like stones
Gave in to soon
Destined for gloom
But hope
Well its within scope
Turn from wicked ways
Graced with treasured days

Stop dragging hurts
Out of the dirt
Seek to start new
Leave behind residue
With strength
Well within arm's length
Turn from worldly vision
It's a personal decision

Commit

Commit
To your game
Be all
You can be
Override
Politics and opinions
Strive
Even if alone
Soar
High don't stop
Let
Them know
You
Require more
Than
They are willing to go
Put
Up good fight
No
Turning back
Do
What's right
In
The long run
You
Will fly
Give
Your best
On
This earthly test

Marching Souls

The dancing of souls has begun
There are many, not just one

Deserted in this savage land
Coming out- taking a stand

With soil that is newly turned
Rising up with a joyous return

Rummage once ripened terrain
Taken for granted yet again

Planting seed along the way
Taking back streets this day

A full moon marked the spot
Where was left to simply rot

Darkness tried to cover light
But they fought with all might

Stood strong in face of battle
Howling sounds of evil cackle

Regardless of current situation
Marched on in firm foundation

Ready to attack, swords in hands
Army flowing at heavenly command

The righteous will prevail
Covered by the Lord's will

Army of darkness will fall
As we all hear the trumpets call

Oblivious

The state of nothingness
Dissolves time and space

Yet you do not know
The emptiness it waste

Energy and lost hope
Every minute is precious

Thoughts come and fade
When oblivious yet conscious

Not seizing the opportunity
To record the moments

Leaving you sitting still
Thinking as opponent

All around life continues
While you wait and wallow

Staring blank with mind full
But no words all shallow

Pen and paper just material
With doubt controlling you

It is a choice to accept
Present is what you do

Perv Epidemic

Today I saw your post
Sinister crimes in this world
So unknown to most
My stomach and head hurled

How can this insanity be
Of evil doing so visible
For all willing to see
Our people, our nation divisible

Story after story comes on
Each more detailed with pain
Society's mind is gone
All for the sinners' gain

Can this really be happening
In the land of free and brave
Young ones held in trappings
Crying out, waiting to be saved

It's a world wide pandemic
Thriving in the underground
Perversion, evil doers epidemic
Ready to be busted, truth found

We shake our heads No
Not my country, not my town
It's time to wake up, let's go
Perv epidemic needs to be shut down

Time

The mist rolls in
Surrounding my skin

Looking out over field
Is this for real

Morning has begun
Another day has come

Pull up my chin
Ready to sink in

Yesterday is now gone
Memories past dawn

Today won't get away
Time will have its say

Petals

Closed petals start to bloom
With the coming of light
Hidden for many hours
Leap forward in delight

Tucked in tight, spreading out
Opening up in gentle stride
Second by second, breath provides
Eyes, ears, limbs come alive

Stretching long, far and wide
Time is precious and cued
Take advantage of the air
And all there is to view

Blowing in the wind
Swaying back and forth
Liberty is to just be
East to west, south to north

Behind Me

Clinging to his leg
As he swung me
Smacking my mom
Is my earliest memory

Out the door he went
Never turned back
Broken home- alone
Mom with two kids, cracked

Did all she could
In this frigid place
Under socialist rule
Hardness in our face

We had so little
Together, but lost all
Found a space- no water
Holes in floors and walls

Mom left me and sister
Daily to do whatever
She'd come back with scraps
Promising it's not forever

I was so young
A toddler, one and half
Sis was around six
Life gave us the shaft

Our tummies ached - grumbled
Tears fell, we struggled
Cold blew, we cried out
Sis and I curled in huddle

Caught the ears of passerbyers
Word was out to find
Fire department came to get
Lifted us to safety, so kind

To the hospital we went
Skeleton thin, starving – neglected
Warm now safe, still afraid
Machines humming – tubes injected

Underweight so fluids began
I was just a wee bit
Sister did the talking
Into strangers hands, we submit

Time went on for us misfits
Plumped up on warm porridge
A new place we were sent
Home was called orphanage

Mom was not able to care
This place was only option
Her family to poor to help
Placed inside, hope of adoption

The home was big – us small
Seperated this boy and girl
Off she went in direction
Life took a hard whirl

Things I remember, some I don't
Although staff and other kids
I felt very much alone
Like a item for highest bid

No idea about mom and sis
I tried to make best of it
Knew when to be seen
And when to spilt

Heard the boots and ran
Crawled below sink pipes
Peeked to see big men
Typical sight and swipe

Little children grabbed – taken
Away they went night and day
I stayed tucked out of sight
Why is it this way?

Years went by, toddler to young
A mere boy inside prime years
Growing up behind stern walls
Coping, living in great fear

Got a chance to visit states
A summer break – holiday
A family agreed to two
Sis and I got a vacay

On the plane, much red tape
To California we flew
These two little orphans
Excited and anxious we grew

But plans had somehow changed
The expected family had a crisis
In mid air we had no clue
Final destination unknown - frightness

We waited in anticipation
Plane landed in free land
Paperwork submitted complete
Escorted off plane holding hands

I was six, sis was twelve
We looked around in wonder
Then we saw a face
Knew it was our foster

Her smile simply said it all
Welcomed us with open arms
We spoke so little English
Yet knew free from harm

Big new place to see
City, roadways and greenery
Sat in back seat peering out
Mind filled with dreamery

All this so very foreign
From where I've been
Surrounded by vast luxury
Made my head spin

So in me and sis settled
Nice people treated us well
Rooms, food, clothes and gifts
Saved us from barred up hell

Not gunna lie, I was wild
Just didn't trust anyone
Each day I had to fight
Couldn't forget what's been done

Days were bad, but good too
Given much care – shown new
These people were kind to us
Knowing all we'd been through

The time went so fast
Places we went, experiences had
This was a life hoped for
Back home was very bad

Here in this safe place
A bond we did make
Not wanting it to end
Days past- started to ache

Had to return holiday over
Both of us begging No
Our hearts, their hearts torn
Law was stern – had to go

To the airport were taken
All sadness upon our faces
Soft words and promises
Hugs and tears, embraces

Towards the boarding ramp
Heads down, holding hands
Me and sis walked to plane
A shout, "we will see you again"

We both turned and looked
I laughed, had heard it before
Sis said "better hurry or we'll die"
Consequences of abuse and war

Back we went, hearts broken
Misery of it all trashing
To have not then have much
Words and actions crashing

Then one day saw her face
The kind one from the states
She came and was here
Just perfect timing, not late

What she spoke was truth
Process tough – the cost great
Yet she powered through
Came to claim, could not wait

Two children touched her heart
With loop holes at every corner
She pressed forward every day
Not giving up on son and daughter

Finally the word became clear
All the obstacles overcome
Us little orphans had grown
Inside communist walls- now done

In the lobby we stood
Staring at her angelic face
Nothing in so nothing out
Doors opened, we ran from place

She scooped us up in arms
Covering us both with a kiss
A new life was brewing
No more time to miss

A glance back I did take
Remembering my prayer book
Turned around ran to door
On the handles I shook

Strange looks I did get
Banging I begged back in
Just for a moment
Grabbed book and out again

Goodbye to the hard life
It hurt me in many ways
Few good times and ones known
But keep praying for your such day

It was freedom for sure
Not easy, many times challenged
Whole new way to live
Loving arms to heal the damage

Adopted at eight, moved to states
A cycle I cannot explain
Thoughts of what had been
Memory getting off the plane

Now twenty-one, and being me
Days I take not for granted
Rescued from depravity
Love has been firmly planted

Alex's story

Sssh!

Hidden symbols now in plain sight
Representing things that are not right
With vows made to serve and honor
Regardless of the pain, willing donor

Hand signals declare they are in
Eye covering, shows sinister grins
Initiation changes the current way
Scorching souls on this very day

What was meant to be secret
Revealed by fame and fortune
Morals amiss, tossed to the wind
Making way for horrific sins

A select few is now many
Hosting elaborate elite gatherings
Celebrations of a dark nature
Power and torture are the flavor

As word spreads it grows bolder
Names and faces of those involved
Shock and anger take center stage
Details leaked, good vs evil waged

Their parties held behind the scenes
Yet not, top class and celebrities
Messing with sinful authority
Innocence taken by sexual immorality

A wicked game they do play
Thinking this is all just okay
Watching blood of victims trickle
Oh how I pray for God's sickle

A blade to come wipe away
All evil from this deranged place
The sssh, stay quiet has to stop
Doers of darkness must all drop

Reach Back

There's a way for all
It's straight ahead
Yet some will fall

Right time and place
Geared up to make
Strive in the race

While you walk track
Remember the fallen
Reach your hand back

A simple "come on"
Will spark inner want
And take beyond

Pit

In that pit of despair
My mind goes everywhere
But no where it should be
As the grip holds on to me

Resist, rebuke, fight to flee
Longing for my destiny
Life with all enticing lies
Flesh and material defy

The pit dark with regret
Lions swat at my head
Threat, the fear grows
In this hole all alone

Cry, scream, pray to thee
To come and rescue me
Take this stronghold away
And set me free today

Chains

When the world's lifeline is unplugged
Know your worth comes from above

You are here to live abundantly free
Not chained to rules and insecurities

When the burden tries to pull you under
Know your purpose, fight like no other

It's time you break this hellish cycle
Hear those chains pop, snap and crackle

Fraud and Find

It's one I've hidden well
So many times given to tell
And yet held it all back
Each time I felt the attack

Why do I cave in shame
Accepting this self blame
When it was not my fault
But brought my life to a halt

This incredible love story
Really did destroy the glory
For it was a web of lies
Cruelest form of goodbye

The steel cages in my heart
Keep me from falling apart
The mask I wear covers hurt
At any price, at any worth

Longing and praying for change
Defeated, cleaned out all wage
Crippled my fiances, ravaged my trust
Gave him all, he left only crust

Hurt so bad I died inside
Felt anything but alive
Yet a tug on my mind
Revealed true love to find

Sinking into depth of word
Is when I finally heard
Time heals all wounds
Get up and lets resume

With the Lord by my side
Able to lay down pride
I was in better hands now
Happiness was fully allowed

Provision did come after loss
When I focused on almighty boss
Taken out of my hiding
Conceding to his guiding

What I thought never would happen
Came to bring my heart passion
I lost much yet gained a man
To love completely cause he can

Was whisked off of my feet
The connection was instantly deep
Now together we do stand
Undeniable, married this woman and man

Loss of what I thought I needed
Pulled me down, left me defeated
But God's plan broke through
And showed me a love true

Anita's story

Eyes

The eyes tell the story
As they are predatory
Not following the law
Striking with both claws

They chuckle and hiss
Blatant attack un-missed
Shame has been brought
No worry, they'll be caught

We watch, listen and wait
Humans trying to create fate
Instead swirling deeper hate
Need to stop before it's too late

The eyes tell of intent
Millions are being spent
Formulating a plan to conquer
Each day evil breathes stronger

Signing laws, destroy and divide
Behind suits and pearls they hide
There's only one ruler of us all
No worry, they'll fall

Watched hands placed under oath
And the deception in the vote
Justice may seem close at hand
By warped women and men

Rant and rave in madness name
Spewing words hostile and blame
The eyes tell they are scared
Running like they just don't care

Hurry up and rush it through
Before finger pointed back at you
The eyes keep telling the story
People are fuming with fury

Boundaries have been crossed
As conformity is being forced
Time for all to lay down swords
Quiet slander and false reward

Just stop the nonsense we're seeing
For we are bleeding human beings
Not much more we all can take
Remember our country is at stake

Vastly

A shimmer of light is all it takes
To catch the eye, curiosity it makes
Calm and stable, flows so smooth
Just like the words lay out truth

A twinkle from sky lays across water
Shines vastly, is a life starter
Make the way clear and straight
Gentle in guidance without debate

Wide canvas of pure beauty
Given freely, no forced duty
Illuminated only by the Son
Praise and honor for all that's done

A serene place of land and sea
How much better could it be
Here now in huge appreciation
Awaiting the final destination

Pandemic

The silence at first is calming
As time goes on, it's swarming
News channels keep repeating
Heartbreak as numbers increasing

Some people do follow the rules
While others dismiss, acting fools
Limited supplies on things needed
Pushing, shoving, manners depleted

Media plays songs of help to come
As big pockets are sharing lump sums
Many pray, asking for healing
To overcome this stifling feeling

And what was is now in past
What will come eagerly fast
Is a better way for us to live
Surrendering all we have to give

Truth Seeker

I have a voice you cannot silence
In the years here walked in compliance
Did what I thought was right
Fought tooth and nail, quite a fight

Orders and laws governed the outcome
Yet I saw not numbers, but someones
With life hanging in the balance
Proving their innocence was the challenge

Took trips into the jail house walls
Hearing caged persons foul cat calls
I walked straight, not looking at
Am on a mission not there to chat

Paper and pen my only allowed tools
The cell houses were filled with rules
I sat there facing chained up people
With nicknames like Dog and Diesel

Time was limited on state's dime
Clock was ticking, talk about crime
I asked questions, waited on replies
Some gave truth, many just lied

Oh this game I knew they played
As they sat claiming were betrayed
Now just the facts was what I seeked
While surrounded by walls of concrete

All eyes stared coldly at me
Anger and desperation, I was enemy
Or so they thought until I showed
That if not guilty I'd go the long road

Gather all evidence to present
Lawyers and judges ways of relent
For not all is what it seems
Some operate within smoke screens

This crazed world is very hard
Like a gambler with losing cards
Not much trust in the system
As many will become victims

Judgment is all around us
Face it straight or simply adjust
But when life is on the line
Bring forth truth, facts to define

I walked those stark corridors
In the hope light will be restored
Bringing in a touch of grace
To the hauntingly solemn space

Moving freely easy for me
Yet those inside it cannot be
Want justice, seeing black and white
But the gray shows what's right

On and on the process can go
Can hinder spirits or truly show
Steps taken are never in vain
Set free innocent, let guilty remain

Battle On

So tired
All the time
From a child
To adult
Body pain
All over me
From my head
To feet

Didn't know
What was wrong
Spoke about it
To everyone
Intense throbbing
Under my skin
Scalp ached
Needles – pins

Missed out
On many events
From my youth
To current
With fatigue
Sleep claimed me
Was restless
Never free

Dizzy spells
Visit to doctors
With no answers
Exhaustion consumed
Me completely
Smothering out life
Trigger points
Sharp knives

Anxiety came
So much pain
My body burned
Head swirled
Thoughts wild
Need great relief
In mind
Was belief

More symptoms
Went to specialists
Pricked and probed
Results showed
Had condition
Myofascial Pain Syndrome
Aka Fibromyalgia
Sent home

Do exercise
Massage and medicine
Will surely help
Yet spent
Worn out
Enter chronic fatigue
To list
Feeling bleak

I learned
To pace self
As weather could
Stimulate pain
Stress too
In any environment
To rouse
Such disquietment

Joined group
To get support
With this disorder
Found ways
To evade
Got some break
No cure
Hope vague

Did research
Methods of cope
Medicine to aid
Pain lessened
Sleep better
Prayed a lot
Cried too
Loosen knots

It's hard
Could be worse
Some can't handle
Extreme suffering
Life taken
But I fight
Hard – strong
All might

I roll
With the punches
Begging it gone
System overload
But not
Done here yet
Still got
Miracle to get

Don't work
Just too weak
To stay alert
Limited in
Daily ways
Keep on going
I'm trusting
And knowing

Some good
Some not so
Take as comes
Make best
I can
When in flare
Pray hard
Heave despair

It is
What it is
Could go on
And on
Just saying
I have battled
Many years
Totally rattled

So thankful
To be here
Despite tough ride
God's love
Does provide
Being still within
Waiting firm
Lifted chin

Ileana's story

Dark Seas Wrath

The dark seas of one's soul
Fills up with bitter cold
Allowing emotions to soar
Truth becomes quickly ignored

A grip that holds on
Pulls down and pushes beyond
Thinking no one cares
Festering a chaotic fear

The dark seas still flow
Forcing under steady and slow
Making a disastrous scene
Got you face down in ravine

A call out, a begging cry
After cutting wrist- don't die
A change in desperate plan
Hoping someone will understand

The dark seas come to cease
Lifting out and bringing peace
Want to try this life again
Needing all family and friends

A release of thoughts of suicide
Feeling a presence has arrived
To guide me back on the path
Love wiped out dark seas wrath

Ember Rolls

Fire in the sky
Seen with naked eye
Glow heats the whole
Losing all self control

Flames dance in air
Flowing free without care
Burning up in refinement
Placing spirit alignment

Layers of ember rolls
Glorious colors – depth unfolds
Above waters so calm
Sending out heavenly balm

Golden angels spread wings
Gliding across blazing springs
Feeling the heat yet knowing
This burning is spiritual growing

Skin

Color of skin
Where hatred begins
Because look different
Brings out ignorant

From another origin
Other than American
Got eyes glaring
The insults blaring

Prejudice in action
Seen by reactions
Outer image distinct
Relations are unlinked

We all bleed
Speaking our creed
Made to love
Not to shove

Skin shouldn't matter
Bond, not scatter
Inner parts same
Bigotry to blame

Unity won't exist
If we resist
Need to change
A mental rearrange

Stop skin focus
Start being gracious
All people matter
Together we gather

Black, white, brown
Tall, short, round
Male and female
We all inhale

Senses

Oh a beautiful sight
Our eyes are blessed to see
Lush green sprinkled with pinks
On display for you and me

Oh the incredible smell
Our noses are sure to follow
As a blend of scents dance
On a field without sorrow

Oh the feeling of touch
Cool yet warm under toes
With tickling blades of grass
On a path all can know

Oh the splendor of taste
Fills our mouths and minds
With sweet pure nectar
From one of a kind

Oh the delight of hearing
Our ears are knowing
The scene ahead is divine
All in majestic showing

Trial and Triumph

Those words shattered my ears
Filled my mind with anger and fear
What everyone dreads I heard clear
Body had invader, cancer was here

Seconds felt long, minutes took forever
A plan devised, hope to get better
Surgery set, mind won't surrender
A journey I will always remember

As medical protocol took over me
With test done, all was ready
Laid me out on a steel gurney
Wondered if I would meet destiny

Time seemed so very long
My frail bones tried to be strong
Thoughts of what could go wrong
Looked up, and out came a song

I wasn't letting the invader win
Not caving into illness' sin
Straightened up with a bold grin
I was not ready for a coffin

Prayer became my only go to
Words came fast, tears it brewed
Talked, sang, wrote it all through
Heart bleed out, God already knew

Word says ask and will receive
Those words true don't deceive
I would not roll over and grieve
Because in Him I do believe

Surgery was quite long and hard
Riddled with disease in body parts
Cut me open, sickness discarded
Healing to come, go full yards

First part of battle was won
Thanking the Father's son
I called on Him, menace be done
Defeat of enemy has begun

Months of treatment I underwent
My body and mind were spent
Many great caregivers were sent
Through it all I was content

Placed in this life changing trial
Had me in a holding for awhile
Grew deeper faith, went extra miles
And the blessings sure did compile

There's no easy way to express it
My world vision changed, I admit
I was not, am not, about to quit
To the light I solely commit

Well twelve years have gone by
Thoughts of his mercy I still cry
My season yielded harsh and dry
Yet it was not my time to die

I stand here this precious day
With only good things to say
Could have ended a different way
However, I was molded like clay

Still got time to encourage
Others with words of peerage
Lay down worldly steerage
And step fully into courage

The trial did not beat me
Rather it allowed me to flee
A bird soaring over open sea
Brought me to Him on my knees

I was given another chance
Not gunna take a back glance
Of what was, instead I'll dance
In triumph, "Yes, I take the stance!"

My story

This collection of poems expresses the trials and triumphs we walk through in life. The good and the not so good situations that hurt our heart, riddle our minds and define our character. In every occurrence, from the smallest to biggest trial, we come to triumph as we press forward in faith. Understanding is not often found, yet what is impossible for mankind is very possible with God.

"All things are possible with God." Mark 10:27 NIV

Acknowledgments:

A huge thank you to the many that supported me in this adventure. The countless hours compiling these poems and testimonies have both touched my heart and humbled me greatly. To my husband, Paul and daughter, Kira, you are my sunshine and thank you for understanding the many times I locked myself away to write or read to you, appreciate you listening.

Thanks Tiffany for your knowledge and guidance. Thanks Ileana for proof reading, editing and honest feedback. Thanks Inez for the text to say "Are you writing?" All those nudges helped me get er done! Thanks to all those that shared a testimony: Claire, Lisa, Kimberly, M, Connie, Alex, Anita and Ileana. Thanks Pauline for a read through and review. Thanks to all my readers, you keep me writing XO.

Greatest thanks to the Lord, without Him it would not be!

Kim Doran is a Christian writer of poetry, self care and short stories. Her passion for people is clearly evident in her written words of rawness in life. She has served in various ministry leadership roles for the past twelve years. Previously, Kim has written two books, LEAD and Pack Your Suitcase. She is currently working on her fourth book.

Kim resides in Jensen Beach, Florida with her husband, daughter and dog. She has a great love of music. Kim is in a worship band that focuses on the community. In addition, she loves to cook, be outdoors and comes equipped with a smile for not a minute is taken for granted.

If interested in having Kim come speak at your church, group or event, she can be contacted at KimDoranSpeaks@gmail.com.

Books are all available on Amazon.com.

www.ingramcontent.com/pod-product-compliance
Lightning Source LLC
Chambersburg PA
CBHW060312050426
42448CB00009B/1793